Visit the Library's On-line Catalog at:
http://www.zionsville.lib.in.us

Call the Library for information on access
if Internet is not available to you.
(317) 873-3149

On-line magazine index with full text at:
http://www.inspire-indiana.net

Killer Whales

Killer Whales

Mark Carwardine

Hussey-Mayfield Memorial
Public Library
Zionsville, IN 46077

First US edition 2001

Published by DK Publishing, inc.
95 Madison Avenue
New York, NY 10016

First published in 2001 by
BBC Worldwide Ltd,
Woodlands, 80 Wood Lane,
London W12 0TT

ISBN 0-7894-8266-5

Produced for BBC Worldwide by
Toucan Books Ltd London

For BBC Worldwide:
Commissioning editor:
Joanne Osborn
Editorial coordinator:
Patricia Burgess
Designer: Lisa Pettibone
Art Director: Pene Parker

For Toucan Books:
Commissioning editor:
Robert Sackville West
Editor: Molly Perham
Designer: Bob Burroughs
Picture researcher: Marian Pullen

Cover photograph: © Tony Stone

Printed and bound in France by
Imprimerie Pollina s.a.
Colour separation by Kestrel
Digital Colour, Chelmsford

Picture credits:

Page 2 Ursus Photography/John K.B. Ford. 6 Tom Stack & Associates/Jeff Foott.
9 Innerspace Visions/ James D. Watt. 10 The Kendall Whaling Museum, Sharon, Massachusetts, USA. 10-11 Sandra Doyle/Wildlife Art Agency.
12 Innerspace Visions/Robin Baird. 12-13 Innerspace Visions/Doug Perrine. 14 Still Pictures/Kevin Schafer, BL; Ursus Photography/ John K.B. Ford, TR.
15 Innerspace Visions/Doug Perrine/ Seapics.com.
16 Innerspace Visions/Phillip Colla, TL; BBC Natural History Unit Picture Library/Jeff Foott.
16-17 Innerspace Visions/Todd Pusser. 18 Sandra Doyle/Wildlife Art Agency. 19 NHPA/T. Kitchin & V. Hurst. 20 Innerspace Visions/Ingrid Visser, TL; Corbis/ Stuart Westmorland, BL.
21 Minden Pictures/Flip Nicklin.
22-23 Hedgehog House/Kerry Lorimer. 24 Ursus Photography/ Finn Larsen. 25 Ursus Photography/Finn Larsen.
26 BBC Natural History Unit Picture Library/Jeff Foott. 27 BBC Natural History Unit Picture Library/Sue Flood.
28-29 Innerspace Visions/Jasmine Rossi. 30 Hedgehog House/Tom Learned. 31 Innerspace Visions/ Amos Nachoum. 32 Sandra Doyle/Wildlife Art Agency.
33 Ursus Photography/Roy Tanami. 34 Auscape/François Gohier. 37 BBC Natural History Unit Picture Library/Jeff Foott.
38 Auscape/D. Parer & E. Parer-Cook. 38-39 Innerspace Visions/ Hiroya Minakuchi. 41 Innerspace Visions/Michael S. Nolan.
42 Minden Pictures/Thomas Mangelsen. 43 Sandra Doyle/ Wildlife Art Agency. 44 Ursus Photography/John K.B. Ford.
45 Innerspace Visions/Robin W. Baird. 46-47 Auscape/D. Parer & E. Parer-Cook. 48 Minden Pictures/Gerry Ellis. 51 Oxford Scientific Films/Doug Allan.
52 Innerspace Visions/Todd Pusser. 53 Hedgehog House/ Barbara Todd. 54 Ursus Photography/Bev Ford. 55 BBC Natural History Unit Picture Library/Jeff Foott, T; Ursus Photography/Roy Tanami, BR.
56 Ursus Photography/Roy Tanami. 56-57 Ursus Photography/ John K.B. Ford. 58 DRK Photo/ Wayne Lynch. 59 Minden Pictures/Flip Nicklin, TR; Innerspace Visions/Robin W. Baird, BL. 60 Ursus Photography/ Roy Tanami. 61 DRK Photo/Jeff Foott. 62 DRK Photo/Doug Perrine. 63 Auscape/François Gohier. 64 Hedgehog House/ Barbara Todd. 65 Innerspace Visions/Michael S. Nolan.
66-67 Tom Stack & Associates/ Thomas Kitchen. 68 Innerspace Visions/Marilyn Kazmers.
69 Innerspace Visions/Ingrid Visser. 70 Tom Stack & Associates/Thomas Kitchen.
71 Olive Pearson. 72 DRK Photo/ Johnny Johnson, TR; Auscape/ D. Parer & E. Parer-Cook, BR.
73 Mark Carwardine.
74 Auscape/Ingrid Visser.
77 Oxford Scientific Films/Mike Hill, BL; Mark Carwardine, CR.
78 Minden Pictures/Frans Lanting. 79 Tom Stack & Associates/Jeff Foott.
80 Auscape/Ingrid Visser.
81 Mark Carwardine.
82 Hedgehog House/Dennis Buurman.83 NHPA/Kevin Schafer. 84 Mark Carwardine.
84-85 Mark Carwardine. 86 Tom Stack & Associates/Thomas Kitchin. 87 Environmental Images/Robin Culley. 88 NHPA/ B. & C. Alexander.
89 Greenpeace/Hewetson.
90 Sandra Doyle/Wildlife Art Agency. 91 Corbis/Brandon D. Cole. 92 Auscape/Wayne Lawler.
93 Oxford Scientific Films/ William Gray.

Contents

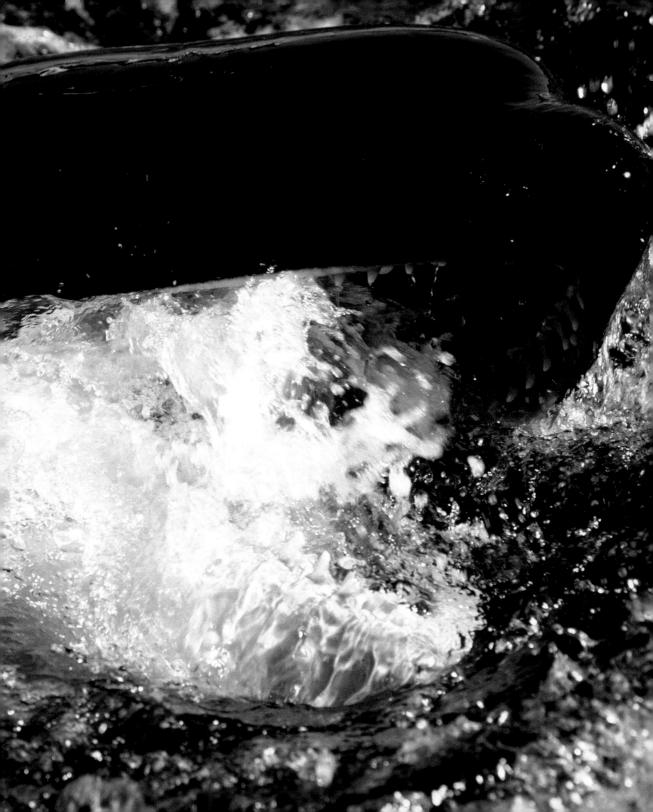

NATURAL HISTORY

NATURAL HISTORY

The first person to write about killer whales was the Greek philosopher and scientist Aristotle (384–322 BC), who correctly classified them as air-breathing mammals rather than fish. But it is only in the past 30 years or so that we have begun to understand the lives and habits of these top ocean predators. Despite the killer whales' fearsome reputation, we now realize that they are complex, endearing and enigmatic creatures, with some intriguing similarities to humans and other highly advanced animals on land. Even researchers who spend almost every day with them in the wild can scarcely believe some of their findings. Killer whales are efficient hunters capable of tackling anything in the world's seas and oceans. They live in close-knit family groups for their entire lives, communicate with one another under water using different dialects, and even demonstrate what seems to be a special affinity with people.

Previous page: Killer whales are capable of tackling animals as large as the blue whale and as dangerous as the great white shark.

THE WORLD OF WHALES, DOLPHINS AND PORPOISES

Whales, dolphins and porpoises belong to a single group of animals known as the cetaceans, from the Latin *cetus* (a large sea animal) and the Greek *ketos* (a sea monster). They form the largest group of marine mammals surviving today, the others being the pinnipeds (seals, sea lions and walruses) and the sirenians (sea cows or manatees).

No fewer than 81 different species of cetaceans have so far been identified and named by scientists, and, as research progresses, it is likely that more will be discovered and added to the list. Bahamonde's beaked whale, for example, was formally named from a specimen found in the Juan Fernandez Islands off the coast of Chile as recently as 1996. Meanwhile, the latest genetic research is revealing that some animals previously thought to be a single species should actually be 'split'. In 1995, for example, the common dolphin was officially separated into two distinct species, now known as the short-beaked common dolphin and the long-beaked common dolphin.

1. The short-finned pilot whale is one of the killer whale's closest relatives.

▷ ART AND MYTHOLOGY

Killer whales have captured the imagination of artists, storytellers, writers and indigenous cultures for many centuries. The earliest known portrayal of them is an ancient drawing carved into rocks in northern Norway that is estimated to be at least 9000 years old. Some 7000 years later, the Nazca people of coastal Peru built temples in honour of kindred killer whale spirits. By contrast, Icelandic sagas and folktales are littered with descriptions of 'evil whales' that attacked fishermen and sank their boats. Over the centuries, killer whales have been honoured, feared and admired by people as far afield as Australia and the Pacific coast of North America. They still play an important role in our imagination and culture, and, most recently, were the stars of the blockbuster *Free Willy* films. The ceramic ceremonial vessel in the form of an orca (shown below) is from the Kendall Whaling Museum, Sharon, Massachusetts, USA. It has a depiction of a human head on its base.

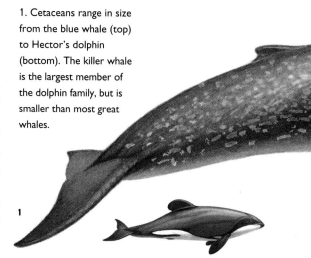

1. Cetaceans range in size from the blue whale (top) to Hector's dolphin (bottom). The killer whale is the largest member of the dolphin family, but is smaller than most great whales.

Whales, dolphins and porpoises come in all shapes and sizes, ranging from the tiny Hector's dolphin, just over 1 m (3 ft) long, to the enormous blue whale, which is almost as long as a Boeing 737. Some of them are streamlined and others are quite chunky. Some have huge dorsal fins, others have no dorsal fins at all. There are those with long, pointed flippers and others with small, paddle-shaped flippers. Some are brightly coloured, or striking in black and white, while others are a relatively drab brown or grey.

Cetaceans also have a wide range of different habits and lifestyles. Some live in freezing cold waters near the Poles, others prefer the warmer waters of the Tropics. Many live in the middle of the deepest oceans, but others prefer to be much closer to shore, while a few even live hundreds or thousands of kilometres inland in rivers such as the Yangtze, the Ganges and the Amazon.

Mammal or fish?

Whales, dolphins and porpoises are mammals, like us, but they are so streamlined, and so well adapted to life under water, that they look more like sharks and other large fishes. They even have similar dorsal fins, flippers and powerful tails. But appearances can be deceptive: the similarities between them are the result of two unrelated groups of animals adapting in similar ways to identical living conditions. On closer inspection, there are actually more differences between them than there are similarities. In particular, most fishes are cold-blooded, they all use their gills to extract oxygen directly from the water, and they lay eggs or give birth to young that can feed themselves. By contrast, whales, dolphins and porpoises are warm-blooded, breathe air with lungs, and give birth to young that feed on their mother's milk for the first few weeks or months of life.

One of the most striking features of any cetacean is the thick layer of insulating fat under the skin, known as blubber, which they have instead of

hair or fur. This makes them look quite different from most mammals, but helps them to keep warm in water, which can draw heat out of the body up to 25 times faster than air.

Classification

Interestingly, there is no real scientific basis for splitting cetaceans into the three groups commonly known as whales, dolphins and porpoises. Broadly speaking, the word 'whale' is used to describe the largest animals, 'dolphin' to describe the medium-sized ones, and 'porpoise' to describe the smallest. But this can be misleading, because some whales are smaller than the largest dolphins, and some dolphins are smaller than the largest porpoises. The situation is even more complicated in North America, where small cetaceans of any kind are commonly referred to as porpoises, whether they are true porpoises or dolphins, or wherever their real zoological affinity lies.

Six 'whales' in particular should really be called dolphins. Despite their names, the killer whale, the

1

short-finned pilot whale, the long-finned pilot whale, the false killer whale, the melon-headed whale and the pygmy killer whale are all members of the dolphin family, the Delphinidae. In many ways, they are anatomically similar to their smaller relatives, which is why they have been placed in the dolphin family. But some scientists believe that, because of their larger size, more rounded heads, blunt beaks and fewer teeth, they should be placed in a separate family of their own. To add to the confusion, these six species are often grouped together as the 'blackfish', which is particularly strange as not all of them are black and, of course, none of them are fish.

1. Like the killer whale, the long-finned pilot whale is a family animal: this one is a young calf.

2. The melon-headed whale looks more dolphin-like than the killer whale, although both species belong to the dolphin family.

2

Toothed and toothless whales

Scientists prefer to split cetaceans into two main groups: toothed whales or odontocetes, which possess teeth, and baleen whales or mysticetes, which do not. There was once a third group, known as the ancient whales or archaeocetes, but its members have all been extinct for millions of years.

The vast majority of cetaceans are toothed whales. There are 70 known species altogether, and they include the narwhal and beluga, all the

1

2

1. The male narwhal's extraordinary tusk is a modified tooth, used as a visual display of strength and sometimes for sparring over females.

2. Dubbed the sea canary by ancient mariners, the beluga is one of the most vocal of all cetaceans.

3. Sperm whales belong to the largest of the two main groups of cetaceans, known as the toothed whales, or odontocetes.

3

dolphins and porpoises, sperm whales and beaked whales. Killer whales also belong to this group. The number, size and shape of their teeth vary enormously. The long-snouted spinner dolphin, for example, has more teeth than any other cetacean with the exact number varying from 172 to 252; at the other extreme, a number of species have only two teeth, and in many females even these do not erupt (so they appear to have no teeth at all). There are as many as 50 teeth in a killer whale's mouth:

⭐ The longest killer whale ever recorded was a 9.8-m (32-ft) male in the western North Pacific.

they are all pointed and sharp, and curved slightly inward for seizing and tearing prey. Toothed whales feed mostly on fishes and squid (although some also take a variety of crustaceans, and a few take marine mammals), and they normally capture one animal at a time.

The baleen whales comprise the remaining 11 species, and make up for their lack of numbers by

Classification of the killer whale

Kingdom:	Animalia (animals)
Phylum:	Chordata (chordates)
Sub-phylum:	Vertebrata (vertebrates)
Class:	Mammalia (mammals)
Order:	Cetacea (cetaceans)
Sub-order:	Odontoceti (toothed whales)
Family:	Delphinidae (dolphins)
Genus:	*Orcinus*
Species:	*Orca*

1. The blue whale is the largest animal on Earth; the calf shown here with its mother is about the length of an adult killer whale.

2. Baleen whales have comb-like baleen plates instead of teeth: these belong to a grey whale.

3. A grey whale feeding on krill, using its furry baleen plates as a sieve.

including most of the larger and more familiar whales, including the blue, humpback, grey and right whales. Instead of teeth, they have hundreds of furry, comb-like 'baleen plates' or whalebones hanging down from their upper jaws. These are tightly packed together inside the whales' mouths, and are covered with stiff hairs that form a sieve to filter food out of the sea water. Baleen whales feed mainly on small schooling fishes, or crustaceans such as krill and copepods, and catch thousands of them at a time.

There are other, more subtle differences between the odontocetes and mysticetes. Toothed whales, for example, are instantly recognizable by their single blow-holes or nostrils, whereas baleen whales have two blow-holes side-by-side.

EVOLUTION

There are still large gaps in our knowledge of the evolution of whales, dolphins and porpoises. Tiny fragments – a few teeth or miniscule pieces of bone – sometimes provide the only tantalizing clues to important links in their evolutionary chain. They are believed to have evolved from a group of furry land mammals called the mesonychids. These strange creatures looked rather like wolves but had hooves like cows and deer. They lived about 60 million years ago, around the ancient Tethys Sea, an area that is now the Mediterranean Sea and part of the Asian subcontinent.

The mesonychids probably spent their lives foraging for fish and other aquatic animals in coastal swamps and estuaries. As they spent more and more time in the water, their bodies began to change. They became more streamlined and developed powerful, flattened tails. Their forelimbs gradually turned into paddles and their hindlimbs wasted away. They developed insulating layers of fat and their body hair began to disappear. To help them breathe at the surface, their nostrils started to move towards the top of their heads to become blow-holes. It is still possible to see evidence of these land-based ancestors in modern whales, dolphins and porpoises. Intriguingly, the bone

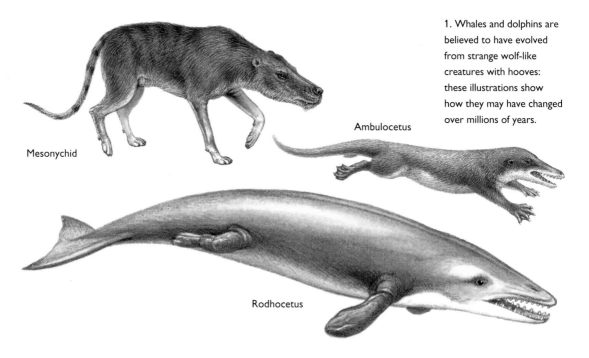

1. Whales and dolphins are believed to have evolved from strange wolf-like creatures with hooves: these illustrations show how they may have changed over millions of years.

Ambulocetus

Mesonychid

Rodhocetus

structure of the pectoral fin or flipper closely resembles an arm and hand with fingers; and, trapped inside the blubber are the remains of pelvic bones that millions of years ago held their hindlimbs.

The first real whale-like animals, archaeocetes, appeared about 10 million years later. They were probably very similar to modern whales, dolphins and porpoises, although they were less well adapted to life in the sea. They may even have clambered back on to land to breed, just like modern seals. The last of the archaeocetes probably died out about 30 million years ago, and by that time representatives of modern whales, dolphins and porpoises were fairly common and widespread. None were exactly the same as the species alive today, but they were unmistakably similar in appearance and in their way of life. By about 5 million years ago most, if not all, modern families of whales, dolphins and porpoises had become firmly established.

The dolphin family appeared around 11 million years ago. Killer whales are believed to be among the oldest members, and probably branched off from the main evolutionary line very early.

Killer whale or orca?

When 18th-century Basque whalers saw killer whales feeding on the carcasses of dead whales, they called them 'whale killers'. Some say that a translator made a mistake and reversed the words, forming the name we use today. Killer whales have had a bad reputation ever since. In reality, they are no different from any of the other top mammalian predators, such as lions, tigers or polar bears, and, from a human point of view, they are far less dangerous than many other animals of a similar size. Many people prefer the other name, orca, but even this has bad connotations.

 HOW DANGEROUS ARE KILLER WHALES?

A warning from the US Navy in the 1970s stated that killer whales 'attack human beings at every opportunity'. Even today, they have an undeserved reputation. In captivity, they have been known to kill their trainers, but this is exceptional: animals kept alone in small concrete tanks are not living natural lives and are often frustrated. Contrary to popular myth, they do not harm people in the wild. There has been one recorded 'attack' – when a surfer was bitten – but he survived after the whale realized its mistake and spat him out. In fact, many people have swum and kayaked with killer whales, with no hint of aggression. No one knows why they should make an exception of humans: perhaps they do not like the taste of neoprene wetsuits, or maybe they feel some kind of affinity with us?

★ The dorsal fin of a male killer whale can be roughly the same height as a man.

It is derived from the scientific name *Orcinus orca* (*orcinus* being a Latin word meaning 'belonging to the kingdom of the dead').

With their predominantly jet-black and brilliant white markings, killer whales are easy to recognize. They have robust bodies and huge dorsal (back) fins: the male's triangular fin is larger than the female's, which is more falcate (curved). They have large, paddle-shaped pectoral (side) fins, or flippers, used for steering and turning in the water, and powerful tails that enable them to reach speeds of 50 km/h (30 mph). There is also a characteristic white patch behind each eye, and a distinctive grey marking, known as the 'saddle-patch', which occurs immediately behind the dorsal fin on the backs of all killer whales. The males of the species can reach a maximum length of 9.8 m (32 ft), with an average

1

2

1. Killer whales are fast and powerful swimmers, capable of catching the swiftest creatures in the sea.

2. With their huge, jet-black dorsal fins, killer whales are easy to recognize.

3. A flock of herring gulls pick up the scraps around a feeding humpback whale off the coast of New England.

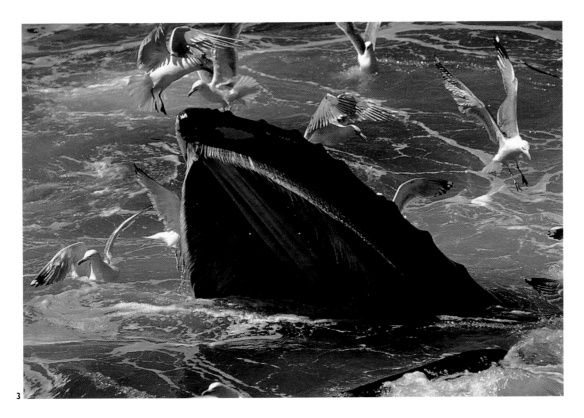

3

of 6.7 m (22 ft). Females can reach 8.5 m (28 ft), with an average of 5.8 m (19 ft). The males weigh about 4 tonnes and the females 3 tonnes, but large males have been known to weigh as much as 9 tonnes.

Distribution

The killer whale is one of the most wide-ranging mammals on Earth, although its distribution is patchy and there are few places in the world where it could be considered abundant. It is most common in cooler waters (especially in the Arctic and Antarctic) and is seen less often in the Tropics and sub-Tropics. It prefers inshore waters close to the coast, and is often found in shallow bays, inland seas and estuaries, but it ranges from the surf zone to the open sea far from land. Unlike some of its larger relatives, it does not undertake regular, long-distance north-south migrations, although its food supply dictates daily, weekly and monthly movements; in polar regions, some populations have to move north and south with the sea ice.

A KILLER WHALE IS BORN

Mating has never been observed in wild killer whales. It is believed that males temporarily leave their family groups, or pods, to seek out females in other groups – or they mate when two or more pods gather together to form a super-pod. More than 100 killer whales may form one of these impressive gatherings, and they can stay together for several minutes or hours at a time. When they eventually split up, and the different pods go their separate ways, the newly pregnant females return to their own families to give birth and raise their calves. The males may never meet their offspring, and certainly do not help in raising them.

The female killer whale has a gestation period of some 15–17 months. Her single calf is born under water, near the surface, and is larger than an adult man: it measures 2.1–2.5 m (7–8 ft) in length and can weigh as much as 180 kg (400 lb). It keeps its blow-hole firmly closed until it reaches the surface, usually with the help of its mother, and then takes its first breath. The youngster initially looks very similar to its mother, although it is not identical. Its saddle-patch is normally darker, and the areas that are white in adults can be quite orange or reddish in colour. However, all its markings are 'correct' by the time it is a year old.

It must be quite shocking for the calf to leave the warmth and safety of its mother's womb and suddenly to find itself in cold sea water. But it soon gains confidence and, under its mother's guidance, begins to explore its new underwater home. The calf is able to swim as soon as it is born, although

1

Previous pages:
A killer whale 'spyhops' to have a look around the Antarctic ice.

1. A young killer whale in captivity is born tail-first: few whales and dolphins have been observed being born in the wild.

2. A young calf feeds on its mother's rich milk: a tricky manoeuvre under water.

its movements are a little awkward at first and it will be several weeks, or even months, before it is able to swim really efficiently. As it learns how to hold its breath for longer dives (some adult killer whales can stay under water for as long as 15 minutes) and how to use sound to find its way around in the dark, it will be able to venture deeper and deeper into the sea. But for most of the time the calf seems to be attached to its mother by an invisible thread. The two animals swim side-by-side and are often touching one another, like a human mother and her child holding hands. This makes it much more difficult for large sharks to single out the calf. Young killer whales are too small and inexperienced to look after themselves, especially if a shark should decide to attack, so they need the protection of their mothers and other members of the pod.

The calf feeds on its mother's milk by holding its tongue against the roof of its mouth to form a kind of tube, and the mother literally squirts her milk inside. The calf is suckled under water, although both mother and baby stay near the surface and come up for air at intervals. Killer whale milk is extremely rich – like a thick cream – and the calf grows quickly. Gradually, it is weaned, and by the time it is one and a half to two years old it is able to feed on solid food and begins to hunt with other

2

1

1. Killer whale calves are suckled under water. As the calf grows older, it looks more and more like an adult killer whale.

2. Killer whales on the attack: trying to separate a mother grey whale from her calf in California.

members of the pod. Gradually, over a period of several years, it will stop drinking its mother's milk altogether. Male and female calves grow at roughly the same rate until they are about 10 years old, but the male eventually outgrows the female.

Growing up

It will be many years before the young killer whale is able to start a family of its own. It has to be at least 10 years old, and possibly as old as 17, before it is able to breed. In some parts of the world the females start breeding at a younger age than the males, but elsewhere they breed at roughly the same age. Mature females reproduce as often as every other year, or as infrequently as every 14

years, but the average interval seems to be about five years. They can continue to reproduce until they are at least 40 years old.

Whether male or female, the killer whale calf will never leave home, even when fully grown. It will spend its entire life in its family group, with its mother, grandmother, half-sisters and half-brothers, aunts and uncles and cousins. All the family members feed, rest and travel together.

Killer whales are long-lived animals and have a lifespan equivalent to that of humans. In the wild, females can live for 80–90 years and males for 50–60 years (males tend to have a much higher mortality rate). On average, males have a life expectancy of about 29 years and females about 50 years. They do not live as long in captivity.

HUNTING AND NAVIGATION

The killer whales' extraordinary strength and cooperative hunting strategy enable them to feed on nearly anything in the ocean; consequently, they have the most varied diet of all cetaceans. They are known to feed on several hundred different animal species, including squid, fishes, sea birds, sea turtles, seals, sea lions, sea otters, manatees and dolphins, as well as animals as large as blue whales. They have even been known to feed on land animals, such as moose and caribou, which are caught while trying to swim across open water.

Killer whale pods normally hunt together and use different hunting methods according to their prey. Some of these prey-hunting techniques are quite involved, and there is evidence that older orcas teach them to younger ones. In the Antarctic they cooperate by tipping sleeping seals and penguins from ice floes into the waiting mouths of other members of the pod. In other parts of the world they even work in shifts to catch seals that hide in underwater caves: they take it in turns to return to the surface to breathe so that there are always some members of the pod ready and waiting when the seals themselves have to come up for air. ▷▷

2

1

 HUNTING ON THE BEACHES

One of the most extraordinary hunting methods used by killer whales anywhere in the world takes place along a remote beach in Argentina. At a place called Punta Norte, in Patagonia, several killer whale pods have learnt how to catch sea lion pups and young elephant seals as they play and splash about along the water's edge. The whales cruise up and down the steep gravel beach, looking for suitable sea lions or elephant seals in the shallows. As soon as they have chosen a likely looking victim, they rush forward, moving so fast that they come right out of the water and on to the beach itself. Most whales and dolphins are in serious trouble when they strand like this, but the killer whales grab their unfortunate prey and then literally wriggle back into the sea. This is such a difficult hunting method that killer whale calves need special training, which can last for several years, to learn how to strand safely. Sometimes the adults in their pod will catch a sea lion pup or young elephant seal and release it again to give the calves some practice – like a cat playing with a mouse. The only other place in the world where this hunting technique is used by killer whales on a regular basis is around the Crozet Islands, in the Indian Ocean.

1. A sea lion pup flees for its life as an enormous male killer whale launches itself on to a beach in Patagonia, Argentina, to seize another pup in the shallows.

1

There is a report from the mid-1860s of a male killer whale with no fewer than 14 porpoises and parts of 14 seals in its stomach.

Each pod tends to have its own favourite food. Those that feed on seals, dolphins and other marine mammals are very careful not to advertise their approach, so they hunt in silence, but the fish-eaters may use sound to coordinate their attack.

Sensing the underwater environment

Killer whales hunt their prey and find their way around under water in ways that are well beyond the scope of our own senses. They can see fairly well in both air and water, but sight is of limited benefit to them because they spend so much of their lives in the dark depths, or in turbid water where visibility is poor. Hearing is far more important: it is effective at night as well as during the day, and does not rely on good visibility. At the same time, sound travels through water nearly five times faster than through air and can be heard over much longer distances. Although killer whales and other cetaceans have lost the distinctive outer ear flaps typical of most other mammals, they do have ears in the form of tiny holes in the skin behind their eyes. They can probably also receive sounds through their lower jaws.

The senses of taste and smell are similar because they are both used to detect chemicals. Sharks, for example, can smell chemicals in the water from a considerable distance away, but killer whales and most of their relatives have probably lost their sense of smell altogether. Taste is more important and is used for detecting chemicals both inside and near the outside of the mouth. Touch is also important. Killer whales have very sensitive skin, and are able to use their dorsal fins, flippers and beaks to investigate unfamiliar objects and to touch one another as a form of greeting or to strengthen social bonds.

Killer whales are also believed to have an extra sense, known as geomagnetism, which enables them to detect the Earth's magnetic field – probably using it like an invisible 'map' to navigate over large distances. Many animals are believed to have this sixth sense, and it may even exist to a limited degree in humans – what we identify in ourselves simply as a 'sense of direction'. But it seems to be particularly well developed in killer whales and other cetaceans, and may help them to navigate their way across the world's seas and oceans.

1. A lone and rather vulnerable Ross seal being harassed by a pod of killer whales in the Antarctic.

2. Hunting a school of herring, in Norway, this killer whale is working with other members of its pod to corral the fish into a tight ball ready for feeding.

2

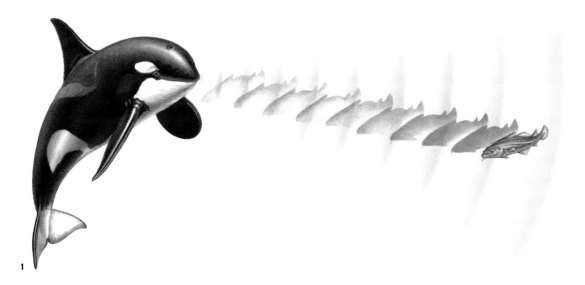

1

 SOUND PICTURES

Killer whales are able to find their way around, keep track of one another and hunt under water without relying solely on eyesight. Instead, they build up a 'sound picture' of their surroundings using a remarkable system called 'echolocation'. Bats, shrews, cave swiftlets, oilbirds and a number of other land-based animals use a similar system to hunt fast-moving prey in the dark. They make special clicking sounds and then listen for the echoes that bounce back. These echoes may come from the seabed, from other killer whales, prey animals such as fishes or dolphins, the underside of a boat, or from any other object in the water. The whales are able to interpret them so accurately that they can identify, for example, the size and shape of a fish, which way it is swimming, its texture, and possibly even its internal structure. It is particularly useful at night and in deep water where there is very little light, or when there is a lot of sand or mud in the water and visibility is poor. Echolocation is actually a form of sonar, but the system used by killer whales is so sophisticated that the human system is little more than a crude imitation by comparison.

1. Killer whales build up a sound picture of their surroundings by emitting loud clicks and listening for the returning echoes.

2. Renowned killer whale researcher John Ford studying sonagrams – visual records of vocalizations for comparisons that cannot safely be made by ear alone.

VOCALIZATIONS

Listening to killer whales 'talking' under water is such a wonderful experience that there is even a special radio station, called ORCA FM, which has continuous live broadcasts from an underwater microphone fixed to the seabed in Johnstone Strait, off northeast Vancouver Island in Canada. Killer whales are highly vocal animals. Their calls, which are normally less than two seconds long, are bursts of pulsed sound: there may be several thousand pulses per second, and the result is a high-pitched squeal or scream. By varying the frequency and timing of these calls, the whales can generate quite a variety of complex signals.

2

Dialect and language

We are still a long way from interpreting killer whale 'talk', although we are beginning to understand what some of it might mean. Each killer whale pod has its own unique range of calls, which are sometimes so distinctive that researchers can recognize them by ear. These are known as 'dialects', and each dialect includes sounds that are unique to a particular pod, as well as other sounds that are shared by different pods. In some ways, killer whale dialects are similar to human dialects. Just as a human family from Scotland sounds different from a Cornish family, one killer whale family will sound different from another.

Individual whales are able to differentiate the calls of their family members from those of other whales, and, since the degree of similarity in dialects seems to be directly correlated to the degree of relatedness, they may even be able to recognize which pods are most closely related to them (a factor that may be important in determining potential mates). But the different sounds do not appear to be given in sequences that resemble syntax, so they probably do not form what we think of as a true language – at least, they do not appear to form the equivalent of a human language – and no call appears to be associated exclusively with any particular activity or behaviour. Nevertheless, the whales can probably convey mood (the emotional state of an individual is reflected in the type of call it chooses to use and in the way it is given), and subtle differences in their calls may enable them to identify one another.

FAMILY LIFE

FAMILY LIFE

Family life is perhaps the most intriguing aspect of killer whale biology. Many animals live in herds, flocks, packs, schools and other groupings, but few are so closely knit and long term as those of killer whales. They travel, feed, socialize and rest in extended family groups, and literally thrive on each other's company. In the early days of research it was speculated that the males were in charge, controlling and mating with their female harems, but the truth is much more unusual and interesting. The females are the family elders, and their sons, daughters, grandsons and granddaughters never leave 'home'. Even strapping 9-m (30-ft) grown-up males live with their mothers for the whole of their lives. In fact, these family groups can be so stable and harmonious that only death or capture can break them apart. Bridging the generation gap, family pods are the key to the killer whales' success.

Previous page: A family, or pod, of killer whales: males, females and calves are all closely related to one another.

LIVING TOGETHER

Many years of research, particularly along the Pacific coast of Washington State and British Columbia, have revealed more about the social structure of killer whales than that of any other whale or dolphin. There are still a great many unanswered questions about the way they organize their family groups, but what has been discovered already is astonishing. It is clear that their social lives are as rich and complex as those of the most advanced animals on land.

The core of killer whale society is the mother-calf pair. The bond between an adult female and her offspring is so strong that neither males nor females ever leave 'home', remaining in the group into which they were born for their entire lives. But the basic social unit, known as the maternal or matrilineal group, is normally larger than just a mother and her calf: it typically contains an older female, or matriarch, and her direct descendants. These might include as many as four generations, with her children, grandchildren and great-grandchildren, and whales of both sexes. The members of a maternal group spend all their lives together, travelling, feeding and resting, and rarely separate for any significant length of time. Maternal groups were previously known as 'sub-pods'.

1. In some parts of the world, almost every individual whale is known to researchers: they will follow the adventures of this young calf as it grows into adulthood and may even observe it with a calf of its own.

Pods, clans and communities

The next level is the pod, which normally consists of one, two or three maternal groups, but may include as many as a dozen. Members of a pod represent a second order of relatedness (an extended family group), with a few closely related mothers and all their offspring. On average, there are between 10 and 20 whales in a pod, but the number varies considerably. Some pods spend most of their time together, but others seem to have grown apart over the years. A young calf, born into the social fabric of such a pod, is cared for by all the pod members, and even adult males help with training duties and babysitting.

Each pod has its own distinct dialect, consisting of vocalizations that are unique to its members, as

1. Killer whale pods vary considerably in size, depending on their home ground, their favourite food and many other factors.

2. Three large males dominate this pod, which was photographed off the coast of British Columbia in Canada.

1

2

well as other sounds that are shared by other pods. The degree of similarity between dialects reflects the degree of relatedness between the different pods. Those with similar dialects belong to the same 'clan', which is the next level of social structure, and are probably descended from a common ancestral group. This means that pods belonging to one clan are probably more closely related to each other than to pods from other clans.

Finally, all the clans sharing the same area belong to a 'community'. It is unclear if the pods within a community are all distantly related, or represent separate lineages, but, intriguingly, pods from different communities never seem to travel together, even if their ranges partly overlap.

THREE DIFFERENT TYPES

Maternal groups, pods, clans and communities are the nuts and bolts of killer whale society. In practice, they are even more interesting and complicated because there are three distinct types of killer whale with three distinct living arrangements.

The two better-known types of killer whale were first recognized by scientists working in the Pacific northwest of Canada and the United States in the 1970s, but studies in other parts of the world suggest that the distinction is universal. They are known as 'residents' and 'transients' and are dissimilar in many ways: they have a different social structure and ecology, as well as different movements, prey

WHERE IS THE FATHER?

While a killer whale pod may contain mothers, sisters, brothers, aunts, uncles, nieces, nephews and cousins, it does not contain any of the fathers. They are living with *their* mothers in other family groups and may never even meet their offspring. It is unlikely that any breeding takes place within a particular pod because all the males and females are closely related, so there would be a problem of inbreeding. Instead, it is believed that calves are the products of matings between males and females from different pods. This arrangement means that young killer whales always come from single-parent families, but they are likely to have several half-brothers and half-sisters to keep them company. Even if the pods of the two parents happen to cross paths again, there would be no way for the fathers to tell which offspring are theirs. Female killer whales are simply too sexually promiscuous for there to be any certainty. Therefore, it is not in the best interests of the males to invest time and effort in helping to raise calves, in case they belong to other males.

1. Much of our knowledge of killer whale family life has been gained through studies in the eastern North Pacific, such as here near the San Juan Islands of Washington State, USA.

1

and behaviour. They are genetically distinct, and recent DNA studies confirm that they have been reproductively separated for thousands of years. Residents and transients never associate with one another and may actively avoid a close encounter. All these differences are strong evidence that they may be separate sub-species in the evolutionary process of splitting into distinct species.

In addition, in recent years, a third possible type of killer whale has been identified. Called the 'offshore' type, it is poorly known but also seems to be significantly distinctive in its appearance, ecology and behaviour.

Resident pods

Resident killer whale pods are much better known than transient pods. Most of the available information comes from nearly 30 years of research in the Pacific northwest of Canada and the United States, but studies in southeast Alaska, Norway and elsewhere suggest that resident-type societies occur in many parts of the world.

Resident killer whales tend to live in the most stable groups. A resident pod comprises as many as 50 or more whales, although there are normally far fewer, and they often split into small sub-groups

1

▷ LIVING WITH MOTHER

The heart of killer whale society is the mother, and the maternal bond is so strong that her offspring never leave 'home'. Even strapping 9-m (30-ft) grown-up males are tied to their mother's apron strings for their entire lives. This is advantageous because the females live much longer than the males and therefore have greater experience. They may survive for 20 years or more after giving birth for the last time, and, as the wise elders of the pod, are able to pass on skills and information to the younger generation. It is not uncommon for mothers, and even grandmothers, to outlive their male offspring.

1. Despite their size, killer whales are extremely agile and often leap out of the water, like other members of the dolphin family.

2. At first sight, the dorsal fins of male killer whales look identical but, on closer inspection, it is possible to identify differences in their shape and scarring.

and disperse over a wide area. Their movements are fairly predictable, normally coinciding with fish migrations, and they seldom stay under water for more than three or four minutes at a time.

Residents have a distinctive appearance and can be distinguished from transients and offshore killer whales at sea. The main feature to look for is the shape of the dorsal fin in the adult female because, although it varies considerably from one individual to the next, it may be sufficient for identification. In residents, the fin tip tends to be more rounded and is positioned over the point where the trailing edge of the fin joins the back; in addition, the leading edge of the fin tends to be straight or curved slightly backwards. Another feature to look for is the presence of an 'open' saddle-patch, in which the grey colour contains various amounts of black.

There are other clues to tell the residents and transients apart: if a group contains fewer than five whales they are probably transients; with more than 10, they are probably residents. Researchers also use vocalizations to tell resident pods from transient ones, because their dialects are so different. Residents have a relatively large repertoire of 7–17 discrete calls, whereas transients have only 4–6, and no calls are shared by the two types.

When they are foraging or hunting, residents spread out to form a broad front and vocalize under water to keep in contact with each other, or to let other members of the pod know if they have found suitable prey. Resident killer whales are often seen in the vicinity of seals, sea lions, dolphins and porpoises, but do not appear to hunt them: they feed predominantly on fish.

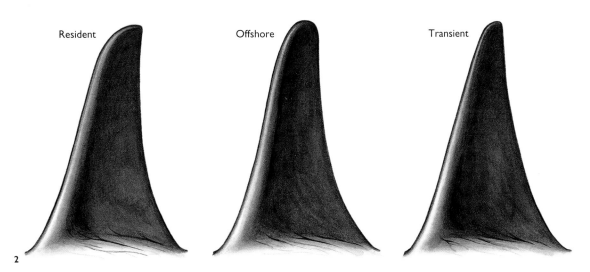

Resident   Offshore   Transient

2

1

Transient pods

Transients are much harder to find and study than residents. They often hug the shoreline when they are travelling or foraging, rarely keep to predictable routes, frequently change course and speed, and have rather erratic patterns of occurrence, rarely staying in one place for more than a few minutes at a time. They live in smaller groups than residents, typically consisting of fewer than six whales, and vocalize much less. They also dive for much longer, staying under water for 5–7 minutes, and sometimes as long as 15 minutes.

Many of these differences are believed to be adaptations to hunting marine mammals. Unlike residents, they have never been observed hunting

⭐ Researchers working in the coastal waters of British Columbia, Washington and southeast Alaska have so far identified more than 720 different resident, transient and offshore killer whales.

or eating fish. Instead, they roam widely in search of seals, sea lions, dolphins and porpoises, foraging in silence and vocalizing only when they have hunted successfully. The rest of the time they keep quiet to avoid detection by their acoustically alert prey: if they were to forage in larger groups, they would be forced to coordinate their activities by vocalizing and this would give away their presence – one possible reason why so few travel together.

Transients do not echolocate in the same way as residents. They do produce irregular 'cryptic clicks', which provide some additional information to help them locate their prey, but these are acoustically camouflaged by all the other noises along the coast. They also listen for the tell-tale sounds made by other marine mammals (a form of passive sonar), and then use the element of surprise in the final

capture. They work together while hunting, as well as foraging, and will frequently cooperate to kill a large sea lion or a whale. The prize is then shared among the various members of the group.

Transients will also chase and harass sea birds, but they rarely eat them. In the Antarctic, they feed on penguins, which have lots of body fat and make a worthwhile meal, but in most other parts of the world they let the birds escape or leave them to die of their injuries. This behaviour is particularly common in young transients and may be a form of play, or a way of learning useful hunting skills.

When they do vocalize, transients all appear to use the same basic dialect. This may be because they have a very fluid social structure, in which group membership frequently changes, so there is little opportunity for unique dialects to evolve.

1. Resident killer whales tend to live in larger and more stable pods, and feed predominantly on fish.

2. A transient killer whale investigates harbour seals at a regular haul-out on Smith Island, Washington State.

2

1

1. A transient killer whale patrols the shallows in search of penguins off the Crozet Islands in the southern Indian Ocean.

Some transient groups consist of several adult females, but most consist of a mother and two or three offspring. However, it is not uncommon for older calves to leave the pod after their mother has given birth to a younger sibling. They may return, some time later, but are not committed to staying with that group for life. This is one of the most important differences between transients and residents. Adult males often travel alone and will occasionally join forces with other transients to form temporary groups.

Offshore killer whales

New research suggests that there may be a third form of killer whale, provisionally designated as the offshore type. First discovered far out to sea, off the coast of British Columbia in Canada, they are the least known of the three types. In appearance, offshore killer whales are most similar to residents, although there are subtle differences, such as in the shape of the tip of the dorsal fin. No precise measurements have been taken, but they seem to be smaller than the other two forms. Their range overlaps with the ranges of both residents and transients, but they do not appear to mix. Offshores are normally encountered in large groups of 30–60 individuals and are believed to feed mainly on fish.

WATCHING AND STUDYING

WATCHING AND STUDYING

Nothing prepares you for a first close encounter with a pod of killer whales. No matter how many times you see them on television, or how often you read about them in books and magazines, in real life they take your breath away. They leave your brain grappling with the improbability that such power and grace could be combined in one creature. They are so inquisitive that it is often hard to tell who is supposed to be watching whom; so engaging that it is even harder to believe that you are in the company of some of the largest and most powerful predators on Earth. Imagine the spectacle of a huge male launching himself high into the air, or a pod of transients hunting a lone seal on an ice floe; the sound of a family of residents in animated underwater conversation, or the sight of a female painstakingly teaching her calf how to hunt. These are the kinds of close encounter that have a dramatic impact on people's lives.

Previous page: Spectacular breach: a killer whale launches itself high into the air head-first, and falls back into the water with a tremendous splash.

A HISTORY OF RESEARCH

The lives of most whales, dolphins and porpoises are still shrouded in mystery. They are among the most difficult animals in the world for scientists to study because they frequently live in remote areas far out to sea, spend most of their lives under water, and then show very little of themselves when they rise to the surface to breathe.

However, despite these difficulties, there have been many astonishing discoveries in recent years, and it is an exciting time to be involved in wild cetacean research. At last, we are beginning to understand the intricacies of the animals' natural behaviour, their diving capabilities, social organization, feeding habits and techniques, and many other aspects of their daily lives.

In the early days of cetacean research, the little information we had came mainly from the dead animals that were washed ashore or killed by fishermen and whalers. Even today, professional postmortems can teach us a great deal about little-known species, such as beaked whales. They are also important when studying the impact of marine pollution, for example, on killer whales and other better-known species. A single carcass can provide an astonishing amount of data, which, when combined with similar data from other carcasses, becomes invaluable.

Since the mid-1800s, an alternative source of information has come from cetaceans kept in captivity. There are some advantages to studying them under controlled conditions: unlike wild animals, they can be observed at close range and

1. In the early days, much of our knowledge of cetaceans was gleaned from dead animals washed ashore. This pilot whale was found in Lincolnshire, England.

for 24 hours a day. Knowing their age, sex and reproductive status, for example, is another major benefit, enabling researchers to study their biology and behaviour in the minutest detail.

However, on moral grounds, many people would argue against keeping cetaceans in captivity for research purposes (or for any other reason). There are also concerns about the actual research itself. Inevitably, an animal in captivity will behave abnormally for at least part of the time, and this can give a distorted picture of its behaviour under natural conditions. Killer whales are a particular problem in this respect because of their immense size and because it is impossible to keep them in their natural family groups. At the very least, conclusions drawn from research on these captive animals have to be treated with some caution.

Venturing out to sea

A great deal of information can be obtained only by studying the animals, wild and free, in their natural environment. Few people took up this enormous challenge until the late 1960s and early 1970s, and it is only in the past decade or two that research into wild whales, dolphins and porpoises really developed into the popular and sophisticated branch of natural science that we know today.

1. A moment of drama as a killer whale attacks a dusky dolphin off the coast of Kaikoura in New Zealand.

2. Researchers observing a killer whale off the coast of Kaikoura in New Zealand.

1

2

The early pioneers concentrated mainly on counting individual animals out at sea. Observers were posted at lookouts on land, in boats, or in light aircraft, and they used relatively simple methods to calculate group and population sizes. These days, population estimates are just as important as ever, but the research has expanded to include a wide range of behavioural and social studies as well.

Modern whale researchers spend long hours patiently observing the same animals day after day, month after month, and year after year. Although they now have access to sophisticated equipment to help them gather information, it is not uncommon to see a researcher using a child's fishing net to scoop up prey samples, or donning goggles, holding his or her nose and hanging over the side of a boat to see what is going on under water.

MODERN RESEARCH TECHNIQUES

In the past decade, the sophistication and variety of information-gathering techniques for wild whale research has grown beyond anyone's wildest dreams. Researchers frequently enlist the help of state-of-the-art equipment and the kind of space-age research techniques that would make NASA proud. Satellites in space, deep-sea submersibles, radio transmitters, high-tech directional hydrophones, complex computer programs, fibre optics, deep-water video probes, DNA fingerprinting and, most recently, the US Navy's submarine tracking system, are now all part of the modern whale researcher's armoury. Killer whales have been studied for more than 30 years off the coast of British Columbia in Canada, and Washington State in the USA, and there are now research projects everywhere from Antarctica to Argentina and from New Zealand to Norway. We probably know more about the social structure of killer whales than that of any other cetacean, thanks to some superb long-term studies pioneered by the late Dr Mike Bigg and his colleagues.

Photo identification

One particular research technique, developed in 1973, revolutionized field studies of killer whales worldwide and has become the key to understanding more about their lives. Mike Bigg realized that individuals could be recognized by the natural

1

1. Researchers off the coast of Vancouver Island in Canada take pictures of two distinctive males for their photo-ID catalogue.

2. The smaller dorsal fin of the female is less distinctive than the much larger fin of the male.

2

DORSAL FIN CATALOGUES

Killer whale researchers can identify individual animals by their natural markings. When they come across a pod, they take a picture of every animal, and this is included in a catalogue of all the whales in their study area, such as this one (right) being prepared by Graeme Ellis. Every pod, and every member of the pod, is given a number. For example, a group of killer whales observed in the Queen Charlotte Islands, Canada, is known as G12 (G2 matriline) and the last time it was seen it had five members: G2, G28, G34, G49 and G53. There are many advantages to keeping a catalogue. It provides a record of individuals, family groups and even entire populations. It helps researchers to follow the whales' movements and their associations with other killer whales. It also ensures that different researchers can compare notes on the same animals.

markings on their bodies: a combination of the size and shape of the dorsal fin, the grey saddle-patch on the back, and the unique patterns of nicks and scars. Each individual is photographed by the researchers and these 'mug shots' help to confirm an individual's identity and provide a permanent record of its existence.

This invaluable research technique is known as photo-identification, or simply photo-ID, and has dramatically improved our knowledge of killer whales over the years. By observing the same individuals continuously, it is possible to follow their movements, map out their home ranges, learn about their special partnerships, work out the

1. Researchers have to spend many days, weeks, months and years in the field before they can understand the intricacies of killer whale life.

2. Killer whales spend only part of their lives at the surface. The greatest challenge for researchers is investigating their lives under water.

1

Many large whales carry distinctive rake-like scars on their bodies, which have been made by killer whale teeth.

sequence and timing of key events in their lives, calculate their average lifespans, and study anything from group stability to the idiosyncrasies of individual killer whales.

The technique has been adopted by researchers working on other whale species, with enormous success. Blue whales, for example, are normally distinguished by the pattern of mottling on the body and the shape of the dorsal fin; right whales can be recognized by the pattern of callosities

1. Photo-ID catalogues have been developed for many species. Researchers use the strange patches of hardened skin on right whales to tell one individual from another.

2. Suction-cup darts, with time-depth recorders attached, are being used to study northern bottlenose whales off the coast of Nova Scotia in Canada.

3. A transient killer whale in Washington State, USA, with a radio tag.

2

3

(hardening of the skin) on the head; and Risso's dolphins can be distinguished by the distinctive scar patterns on their bodies.

Satellite telemetry

Unlikely as it may sound, the answers to many of the more perplexing questions about whales probably lie in space – or, to be more precise, they lie in satellites orbiting in space. The idea of tracking whales by satellite may sound like science fiction, but it is a technique that has already been tried and tested on several species with considerable success. Researchers normally use a modified gun or crossbow to fire a small, battery-powered

1. By using directional hydrophones (underwater microphones) researchers can study the underwater vocalizations of killer whales.

transmitter into the thick blubber of the whale's back. This beams signals up to communications satellites, which relay the coded information back to receiving stations on Earth. As satellites continually scan the entire surface of the Earth, the study animals can be tracked wherever they go. The information is then sent to researchers sitting in front of their computers in offices that may be hundreds or thousands of kilometres away from the whale itself.

These days, in addition to signalling a whale's movements, satellite transmitters can provide a great deal more information as well: swimming patterns, dive depths and heart rate, environmental conditions such as the surrounding water temperature and pressure, and many other things.

Listening for whales

Our ability to learn about whales simply by listening to the sounds they make is no longer science fiction but real science fact. An astonishing amount of information can be obtained by using sophisticated underwater microphones, called hydrophones. This is undoubtedly a challenging area of research – in some ways, rather like trying to find out what goes on in New York merely by dangling a microphone from the top of the Empire State Building – but it is revolutionizing our knowledge about killer whales and other species.

It may even be easier to count whales by listening for them rather than by the age-old technique of looking for them. Researchers at Cornell University in Ithaca, New York, have developed a sound-sensitive 'acoustic telescope' that seems to be better at spotting whales than human whale-watchers are. The 'telescope' consists of 16 hydrophones attached to a line about 1.6 km (1 mile) long, which is towed behind the research vessel. By listening carefully to the sounds the whales make, it is possible to identify the species, to distinguish individual animals and to work out what they are doing.

DNA fingerprinting

Do different calves with the same mother have the same father? Do the fathers have anything to do with their upbringing? Are individuals that spend a lot of time together related? These and many other intriguing questions have been answered just by examining a small piece of a whale's skin. More accurately, it is the genetic material, or DNA, in the skin that is so revealing.

The clever detective work involved in interpreting this highly complex information is called DNA

 JOHNSTONE STRAIT

Killer whales have been studied in Johnstone Strait, between Vancouver Island and mainland British Columbia, since 1970. This was one of the first, and is now one of the longest-running, research projects into wild whales. Over the years, researchers have identified and studied more than 700 individual killer whales in the region stretching from Washington State, through Johnstone Strait and into southeast Alaska. Every animal has a personal file, containing mug shots and an abundance of information on its life. The researchers locate the whales by boat, often with the help of an underwater microphone, and whale-watchers, local boaters and volunteers living along the waterfront report sightings to them. Every time a pod is encountered, all the individuals present are identified and their vocalizations are recorded, along with a variety of other information, from their travel route and swimming speed to mixing within the group. Here researcher John Ford uses a hydrophone.

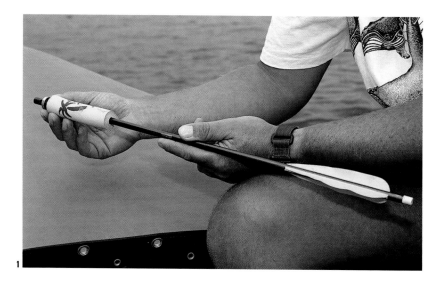

1. A whale dart, used to retrieve small plugs of skin for DNA analysis.

2. When a whale leaps clear of the water, it is said to be breaching; juveniles in particular often attempt more adventurous twists and turns.

fingerprinting, and it is already proving invaluable in wild whale research. The DNA itself is a kind of instruction manual for the design and assembly of the body's proteins. Every cell in an animal's body contains an exact replica of this manual, and almost all the 'pages' go to making the animal what

⭐ Researchers take a tiny sample of skin, and then do a simple genetic test to tell whether a young whale is male or female.

it is – a harbour porpoise, a long-snouted spinner dolphin, a humpback whale, a killer whale, and so on. But the small number of pages that are left help to distinguish one individual from another. Just as one person's fingerprints are different from everyone else's, no two animals have exactly the same DNA. Most importantly, the degree of similarity in the DNA of two different animals reflects the degree of their relatedness.

Researchers have now examined the genetic material from nearly 300 killer whales along the west coast of northern North America, from British Columbia to Alaska, and many more have been examined elsewhere in the world. A major advantage of this line of research in killer whales is that it provides a new tool to determine the gender of calves, which are otherwise difficult to sex unless they roll over to show their undersides.

INTERPRETING BEHAVIOUR

Killer whales are very active and some of their more impressive and energetic displays take place at the water's surface. They roll on to their sides or back and slap the water with their flippers, fins or tails. They lift their heads above the surface, apparently to have a look around, and sometimes they leap high into the air, landing back in the water with a tremendous splash. (This is known as breaching.)

A great deal of research has been done on these displays and, at last, we are beginning to unravel some of their secrets. It is likely, however, that a particular display will have different meanings at different times. Slapping the surface, for example, may be a form of courtship display, a way of signalling across great distances under water, a technique for herding fish or dislodging parasites, a show of strength or a challenge – or, in some cases, it could simply be for fun.

It is difficult to imagine that certain forms of behaviour observed in killer whales can be anything more than exuberant play. They chase one another, jump in the air, launch into bursts of erratic swimming, and twist and turn in the water. If they hear a passing boat or ship, they sometimes

2

go out of their way to investigate or swim along-side. Some of them seem to enjoy the company of people, and even play with pieces of seaweed, pebbles and other objects in the sea, carrying them around in their mouths or balancing them on their flippers. But there is little doubt that play also has an important role in their lives, and some of these activities inevitably have logical explanations. In young animals, for example, it forms part of the learning process, and in adults it may help to strengthen social bonds.

Killer whales and other cetaceans do not sleep as other mammals do, but take short catnaps. Resting killer whales move very slowly and methodically, usually staying close together and sometimes even touching one another. They breathe synchronously

1. Spyhopping is when a whale pokes its head above the surface of the water, apparently to have a look around. Killer whales can see both above and below the surface.

2. (opposite) Lobtailing is the forceful slapping of the flukes against the surface of the water. Also known as tail-slapping, it is done while the main body of the whale lies just beneath the surface.

in shallow breaths, and always remain silent. Sometimes, one or two whales will 'ride shotgun' on the periphery, keeping watch and herding the other pod members away from any obstacles in their path.

Intelligence

Are killer whales as intelligent as we would like to believe they are? They certainly *seem* to be intelligent: they have large brains, live in complex societies, help one another in times of trouble, learn from their experience, are often playful, and sometimes even seem to enjoy human company. But no one really knows whether they *are* intelligent, for two main reasons.

First, it is difficult to define exactly what we mean by 'intelligent', and even more difficult to take meaningful measurements. It is hard enough with humans, let alone killer whales, which cannot talk or work with tools such as pens or computers. Second, any discussion of intelligence tends to be highly subjective: after all, we have only a human perspective, and can scarcely imagine what goes on inside another animal's mind.

The fact that killer whales have embarked on a completely different evolutionary path from our

1. Blowing, or spouting, is when a whale breathes out and a cloud of water droplets is produced above its head.

1

Some killer whales have a special greeting ceremony, rubbing and rolling against one another when they are reunited after a separation.

own makes any comparison with humans almost impossible. Human intelligence suits our own way of life and, consequently, a large part of our brain deals with the use of hands to write, paint, sculpt, build or manipulate objects that exist outside our own bodies. If we were to judge killer whales on these terms, they would fare badly. But their intelligence suits a completely different way of life, and may concentrate instead on social skills, emotional self-control and other more spiritual and philosophical requirements. Taking these factors into consideration, many people would argue that killer whales are far more intelligent in their world than we are in ours.

WHALE-WATCHING

Watching killer whales and other cetaceans in the wild is an unforgettable experience. Who could remain untouched by the sight of a 9-tonne male launching himself high into the air, the drama of a pod corralling a shoal of herring in a remote Norwegian fjord, or the sound of a close-knit family group 'talking' to one another under water? These are the kinds of close encounter that change people's lives. But to guarantee the best experience involves a little advanced planning and preparation.

Finding the animals at sea

People with a lot of experience at sea instinctively recognize the tiniest clues when they are looking for killer whales and other cetaceans. They are trained to register the slightest movements and splashes that give their presence away. With killer whales, for example, the first clue might be a blow or spout. This is not as visible as in many of the larger baleen whales, but it can be distinctive in some weather conditions. It may look like a flash of white (especially against a dark background) or a more gradual puff of smoke. Alternatively, you may see the enormous triangular dorsal fins of the males, or even the smaller, falcate fins of the females. Splashes are also good clues: they can be caused by a whale breaching, flipper-slapping or lobtailing. Anything suspicious is worth investigating.

Do not forget to look everywhere: in front, behind and to both sides. Scan the horizon with binoculars and use the naked eye to check nearer the boat. It is amazing how often people miss whales surfacing surprisingly close to them because they are too busy looking far out to sea. The golden rule is to be patient because even in areas with well-known killer whale populations, it may take a while to track them down.

1. Porpoising is when a whale leaves the water at each breath while travelling at speed. This is thought to reduce friction on the body, thus conserving energy.

2. Whale-watchers enjoy a close encounter with a killer whale off the coast of New Zealand.

2

Responsible whale-watching

It is important to cause as little disturbance as possible when watching killer whales and their relatives, and we also have a responsibility to help them benefit from whale-watching through education, conservation and research. Educational whale-watching trips help to raise public support for killer whales in many ways. They make people more sympathetic towards the animals and towards marine conservation. After a close encounter with a whale, the state of the marine environment is no longer just a general problem somewhere out in the ocean: it becomes a direct threat to the animals the whale-watchers have just observed. Oil spills, marine debris, whaling, destructive fishing methods, over-fishing and many other issues become very real.

Whale-watching can also make a valuable contribution to research. Although there are plenty of well-qualified and willing researchers around the world, the cost of owning and running a research boat is often prohibitively expensive and a lot of important work never gets done. Whale-watch operators can help to solve this problem by undertaking simple studies themselves, and by assisting with more complex studies that are carried out by professional cetacean biologists.

Simple research projects suitable for commercial whale-watch operators include keeping a detailed logbook, building up a catalogue of local animals through photo-identification, and reporting unusual sightings to local biologists and research organizations. More involved research projects can be undertaken by providing professional biologists

1

1. When whale-watching, it is essential to understand the animals' behaviour in order to cause as little disturbance as possible.

2. Where to watch killer whales: some of the better-known sites around the world.

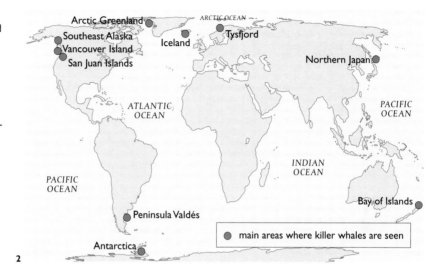

main areas where killer whales are seen

2

with platforms for research. The biologists act as on-board naturalists, help to find the whales, provide informative and entertaining commentaries, and answer questions from clients. In return, they have free passage on every trip to do their research, and might even receive a percentage of the ticket price towards their research costs.

Where to watch whales

It is possible to encounter killer whales in seas and oceans almost anywhere in the world, but they tend to have localized pockets of abundance and may be present only at certain times of the year. It is therefore necessary to go to the right place at the right time to have a reasonable chance of finding them.

In the USA, southeast Alaska is a wonderful place to watch killer whales in a truly spectacular setting. It is also the best place to see humpback whales doing the unimaginable: fishing with nets made of bubbles. Tours leave from many different ports, including Gustavus, Juneau, Petersburg, Seward and Ketchikan, throughout the summer. There is a wide range of trips on offer, from kayaking to large-scale cruises, and from day trips to two- or three-week wilderness excursions. Killer whales can also be seen around the San Juan Islands of Washington State during the summer. June and July are generally considered to be the best months. As well as regular boat trips, San Juan offers some wonderful opportunities to kayak with the whales.

In Canada, killer whale sightings are more or less guaranteed on commercial whale-watch trips in Johnstone Strait between the Canadian mainland and northern Vancouver Island. Trips leave from the little village of Telegraph Cove, and a number of other communities on Vancouver Island. They run throughout the summer, and frequently encounter Dall's porpoises and other cetaceans as well.

Peninsula Valdés in Patagonia is internationally renowned for its killer whales. Punta Norte, on the tip of the peninsula, is a regular hunting ground for several different pods. There is a viewing area overlooking a long stretch of beach, from which they can sometimes be seen stranding themselves to catch young sea lions and elephant seals. Peak activity is usually in March. The region is also known for it southern right whales, which breed in two bays on either side of the peninsula. They can easily be seen during the southern winter (mid-July to November) on day tours from the towns of Puerto Madryn, Trelew and Puerto Pirámides.

Whale-watching is relatively new to Iceland, but there are already more than a dozen operators working from almost as many different towns and villages all around the coast. Killer whales are most common around the Westmann Islands, along the

1

 BEACH RUBBING

A common and intriguing behaviour observed in some of the killer whales living in Johnstone Strait, British Columbia, is beach rubbing. They visit certain beaches in the Robson Bight (Michael Bigg) Ecological Reserve and then rub themselves on the pebbles close to shore. The whales seem to take it in turns at their favourite 'rubbing beach': while one animal swims closer to shore and disappears from view, the others patiently wait at the surface. Why they do it is something of a mystery, but it may be that they enjoy the tactile stimulation.

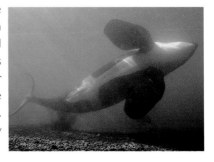

Snaefellsnes and Reykjanes peninsulas, and in the Eastern Fjords, but they can be encountered almost anywhere. The main season is during the summer, when it is possible to go whale-watching in the golden light of the midnight sun.

Another killer whale hotspot is the Tysfjord area in northern Norway. Every autumn, hundreds of killer whales arrive to feed on herring, and the sight of the large, carefully coordinated pods corralling the fish is unforgettable. Unfortunately, the whale-watching season is restricted to about a six-week period before the end of November, and even then, there are only 4-6 hours of daylight each day. The whales normally stay for the winter, but after November there is too little daylight to watch them.

Antarctica is perhaps the ultimate whale-watch destination. It is an expensive place to visit (the only way to get there as a tourist is aboard a cruise ship),

but it offers more whales and dolphins than most people will ever see anywhere else in the world. With huge numbers of penguins, seals and other wildlife as well, and a spectacular icy setting, any visit there is likely to be the trip of a lifetime. Most Antarctic cruises leave from the southern tip of South America (normally Ushuaia in Argentina, or Punta Arenas in Chile) and pass through several different marine habitats in the space of two or three weeks. The inshore waters of Tierra del Fuego (and South Georgia and the Falklands, if they are included in the itinerary), the high seas of the Drake Passage, and the region of broken ice around the Antarctic Peninsula itself each have their own cetacean specialities. Killer whales can be seen in any of the three main habitats, although they are normally encountered hunting between the ice floes along the Antarctic Peninsula.

1. Killer whales are particularly common in the cooler regions of the world, and watching them against the spectacular backdrop of southeast Alaska can be a life-changing experience.

2. A training session for young killer whales learning to hunt sea lion pups in Patagonia, Argentina.

2

KILLER WHALES IN TROUBLE

KILLER WHALES IN TROUBLE

Since time immemorial, killer whales have had a reputation as bloodthirsty and dangerous, and they have suffered as a result. In the first century AD, the Roman scholar Pliny the Elder described them as 'enormous masses of flesh armed with savage teeth', and, as recently as 1973, US Navy diving manuals warned that they are 'extremely ferocious'. But humans are far more dangerous to killer whales than the other way round. We should be the ones with the bad reputation. We capture them in the wild and then keep them in small concrete tanks, we pollute their ocean homes, compete with them for fish, and threaten them in so many ways that conservationists now fear for their future. Killer whales are not endangered in the way that, for example, giant pandas, black rhinos and tigers are on the verge of extinction, but they face so many threats that urgent action needs to be taken to make their future more secure.

Previous page: Keiko enjoying relative freedom in a purpose-built sea pen in the Westmann Islands, Iceland.

KILLER WHALES IN CAPTIVITY

Killer whales have been kept in marine parks and zoos for about 40 years. They are trained to jump through hoops, balance balls on their heads, 'kiss' their trainers, perform synchronized leaps and somersaults in specially choreographed shows, and do many other tricks for the millions of people who flock to see them every year. Their owners argue that the animals 'enjoy' the shows, and are lucky to be safe from predators, pollution and other threats in the wild. They point out that, as the stars of marine parks and zoos, they are worth a great deal of money and, directly or indirectly, provide thousands of people with secure jobs. They also claim that captive animals encourage members of the public to take an interest in the conservation of their wild relatives.

Most conservation and animal welfare groups are strongly opposed to keeping killer whales in captivity. Above all, they argue that it is immoral and cruel to keep such large, family-orientated, wide-ranging animals in concrete tanks. They point out that the captive animals are sometimes so

2

1. Every day, somewhere in the world, captive killer whales are performing carefully rehearsed shows in front of huge audiences.

2. A quiet moment, when it is impossible not to wonder what the whale is thinking.

unhappy that they swim round in circles, stop vocalizing, and become aggressive or depressed. They also argue that a marine park or zoo can make money and provide jobs without killer whales: Monterey Bay Aquarium in southern California has no whales at all, yet, in terms of revenue and visitors, it is the most popular aquarium in the USA.

Dying to entertain

Many years of breeding attempts have failed to produce a sustainable population of killer whales in captivity, and, although some have been born in marine parks and zoos, breeding programmes around the world have resulted in more deaths than births. The reasons for this probably range from general poor health and complications during birth, to a lack of experience in looking after newborn calves. The vast majority of animals on display have been taken from the wild. It is now illegal to capture killer whales in some countries (the United States and Canada banned it in 1976, and Iceland did the same in 1989), but it is still allowed in other parts of the world.

Wild killer whales were caught in Japan quite recently. On 7 February 1997, a pod was passing through Japanese waters, when all 10 family members were captured by fishermen in Taiji. They were driven into Hatajiri Bay and examined by marine park personnel. The five largest animals were released, but the others (three young males and two females) were taken into captivity by

1. Killer whales are particularly large animals to keep in captivity.

2. Captive killer whales are often trained to perform a variety of tricks – deemed humiliating by animal welfare groups – to entertain their human admirers.

several different Japanese marine parks. The Taiji Whalers Union was paid more than $700,000 for them. Later, two of the five captive whales died in their new homes: one was a pregnant female, who miscarried. There are rumours that a third has since died, too. Japan once had a healthy population of resident killer whales, but so many have been killed and captured over the years that very few of them are left.

The places holding captive killer whales include a bewildering range of establishments, from badly run zoos with poor treatment to professional marine parks with the best care and attention that money can buy. But almost all their killer whales have been taken from the wild and separated from their close-knit family groups. Most are forced to live alone, or with unfamiliar company such as dolphins or seals, and most are kept in small and featureless concrete tanks, in chlorinated water,

1. Life alone in a concrete tank is far removed from family life in the wild.

2. A killer whale is rewarded with dead fish at the end of a show.

▷ CATCHING A WILD KILLER WHALE

The technique used to capture killer whales has changed over the years. In the 1960s, captors used a range of different nets to encircle the animals, and in some parts of the world even tried harpooning them. Not surprisingly, the whales sometimes died in the process. In recent years three main methods have been employed. The first is waiting for a pod to swim into a narrow, shallow-water inlet, then stringing a net across the mouth to capture the entire family. The second involves encircling one or more whales with a purse seine net: as the net is drawn tighter, they will often lie still at the surface and accept their fate. The third method, which is sometimes used in Japan, is using lots of boats and noise to frighten the whales and drive them ashore.

where they can no longer hunt or hear the sounds of the sea. To make matters even worse, they have to eat dead fish and cope with hordes of noisy people watching them day after day.

More than 135 killer whales have been kept in captivity worldwide since 1961. Most of them were captured as young animals and yet 74 per cent have died. Life in captivity is so stressful that, while males can live as long as 60 years in the wild, and females up to 90 years, captive animals have an average lifespan of just five years. The figures speak for themselves.

Poor education

One of the main arguments for keeping killer whales in captivity is education. The protagonists claim that captive animals act as ambassadors for their wild relatives, providing the only opportunity most people will ever have to experience them in real life. But animal welfare groups argue that few captive facilities make a genuine effort to educate the public, so the real benefits and spin-offs for their wild relatives are very limited. Choreographed shows are particularly contentious: trainers argue

2

1. Watching whales in the wild is a far better alternative to watching them in captivity.

2. Keiko, star of the film *Free Willy*, with some of his human admirers.

that they are educational, and keep the animals physically and mentally fit, but animal welfare groups regard them as cheap entertainment done purely for profit.

Many experts argue that it is not essential to see killer whales in real life in order to appreciate them, pointing out that it is possible to learn about the Moon without actually standing on it. So while a real, live animal is more likely to trigger the emotions than words, photographs or films, these could be strong second bests. Meanwhile, there are some exciting possibilities for the future, including computer technology that could simulate virtual-reality encounters with killer whales where they really belong – in the oceans, wild and free.

Campaign for captive orcas

Given that killer whales are completely unsuited to life in captivity, it is not surprising that animal welfare and conservation groups on several continents have been campaigning for years for the capture of wild killer whales to be banned in every corner of the world. Where appropriate, they would also like to see animals already in captivity being released. Keiko, star of the film *Free Willy*, is already on his way to freedom, but there are several other possible candidates for future releases.

One of these is Corky, a female killer whale held at Sea World in San Diego. This is her 32nd year of imprisonment, and she is now the longest surviving killer whale in captivity. Corky holds another record, too: on 28 February 1977, she delivered her first calf, a male, which was the first live killer whale to be born in a concrete tank. Back in the wild, Corky's family lives on. Her pod once had 18 members, but six of them were captured in 1968, and all six are now dead. Corky herself was among six more taken a year later. The five family members taken with her are also now dead. Time is running out, but the Free Corky Campaign is calling for her return to the wild while she still has the chance to live at least part of her life naturally.

⭐ Even after years of separation, captive killer whales remember the dialect of their original pod, but also learn the dialects of any other killer whales in the tank.

2

1

 FREEING KEIKO

Keiko, star of the 1993 film *Free Willy*, was captured in Iceland in the late 1970s, when he was about two years old. He touched the hearts of millions of people as a Hollywood star, but there was a public outcry when cinema-goers realized that he was still living in a small concrete pool in an amusement park outside Mexico City. This prompted the formation of the Free Willy Keiko Foundation and a massive worldwide fundraising effort. In 1996 Keiko was transferred to a purpose-built tank in Newport, Oregon, on the west coast of the United States, where he began the first-ever rehabilitation programme for a killer whale. In 1998 he was ready to go back to Iceland, and was transferred to a large netted enclosure in the Westmann Islands, off the south coast. He has since been allowed to roam further afield, now that the bay harbouring his original enclosure has been netted to prevent his escape into the open sea, and this is where he now lives. Only time will tell whether he will ever be released back into the wild to fend for himself, but there is mounting pressure for him to be set free.

1. Keiko with a trainer at his temporary home in Newport, Oregon in the USA.

CONSERVATION ISSUES

Killer whales are not recognized as being an endangered species, but there could be as few as 100,000 of them worldwide, and they face many different threats. Unlike most of their larger relatives, they have never been especially prized for their meat or oil, but significant numbers have been killed in the past. More than 2000 were taken by Norway during the period 1938–81, for example, and the Japanese took more than 1500 from 1946 to 1981. Russian whalers have also caught them, in Antarctica, killing an average of 26 animals every year from 1935 to 1979, and then an incredible 916 animals in the 1979–80 season. They may still be

hunted occasionally by native fisheries on isolated islands in some parts of the world, and, of course, small numbers continue to be taken into captivity.

Ultimately, environmental problems, such as global warming and the depletion of the ozone layer, could have a detrimental impact on killer whales and their relatives. Exactly how they might affect the world's seas and oceans, and their inhabitants, no one really knows. There is intense debate about how global warming may be causing sea levels to rise, and there are fears that ozone depletion could harm plankton and thereby affect the entire ocean ecosystem. More specifically, killer whales face three main threats: conflicts with fisheries, pollution and habitat degradation.

1. Killer whales and fishing boats share the same seas and oceans throughout the world.

2. A Japanese whaling factory ship with a pod of killer whales in the Southern Ocean in the early 1990s.

2

rockets and depth charges in an effort to rid the country of killer whales. More recently, in the mid-1980s, Alaskan fishermen in Prince William Sound resorted to explosives to stop them stripping commercial longlines of blackcod and damaging the fishing gear in the process. Even today, in some parts of the world, disgruntled or fearful fishermen undoubtedly fire bullets and dynamite at these 'troublesome' predators.

There is no doubt that killer whales can be a nuisance to certain fisheries. They sometimes wait near fishing boats and snatch fish from the nets, causing expensive damage in the process, and they will even take fish from hooked lines. But they can also help the fishermen: salmon nets are sometimes set in the path of foraging killer whales, for example, and mackerel boats sometimes use them to find schooling fish.

Whether or not they compete for fish stocks is another matter. Marine ecosystems are extremely complex, so it is actually very difficult to calculate the impact of killer whales on fisheries. But limited evidence suggests that, in some places, fishermen and whales are taking entirely different species of fish. More importantly, the scarcity of fish may be the result of over-exploitation, and the whales are simply being used as scapegoats for badly managed fisheries. The sheer scale of many modern fisheries is frightening, and they over-exploit fish stocks with scant regard for the future health of the world's oceans. In truth, the whales themselves are likely to be suffering from the depleted stocks.

Like most whales, dolphins and porpoises, killer whales face a variety of other threats from fisheries.

Conflicts with fisheries

In some parts of the world, fishermen have had clashes with killer whales. Herring and mackerel fishermen in the Faeroe Islands, salmon fishermen in British Columbia and Washington State, and blackcod fishermen in Alaska, all consider killer whales to be competitors for fish or accuse them of frightening the shoals and making them impossible to catch.

Some fisheries have taken drastic action in the past. Perhaps the worst example was in Iceland, in 1956, when the local Greenland halibut fishery persuaded the US Navy to use machine-guns,

1

Since the 1950s, the staggering growth of the fishing industry and the introduction of increasingly destructive fishing methods have spelt disaster for cetaceans around the world. Hundreds of thousands of them – maybe even millions – die slow, lingering deaths in fishing nets every year.

Drift-netting is one of the worst culprits and, indeed, is probably the most indiscriminate method of fishing that has ever been devised. Hanging in the water, unseen and undetectable, drift nets are carried freely with the ocean currents and winds. Dubbed 'walls of death' or 'curtains of death', they catch everything in their path, from sea birds and turtles to whales and dolphins. Each net can be as long as 50 km (31 miles), and although lengths of over 2.5 km (1.5 miles) are now illegal, there are more than enough of them floating around the world's seas and oceans at any one time to circle the Earth at the Equator.

Gill nets are similar to drift nets in design, although much smaller, and pose another threat. As they are relatively inexpensive, these deathtraps are used along coastlines and in major rivers worldwide, from New Zealand and Sri Lanka to Canada and Britain. Tens of thousands of small cetaceans are believed to drown in them every year.

Unfortunately, there are no easy solutions to most of these conflicts. The fishermen's needs, as well as those of the killer whales, have to be taken into consideration. In some cases, a simple modification of the nets or the fishery management system can have a positive effect. Educational programmes for fishermen, and newly developed devices that alert whales and dolphins to the presence of nets, may also work in some situations. But when it comes to overfishing, there is no escaping the fact that much more drastic action, such as seasonal closures of some fisheries or changes in fishing techniques, may be the only effective solution in the long term.

Marine pollution

Some experts predict that pollution could be the most serious threat to whales, dolphins and porpoises in years to come. It is a silent, insidious and widespread killer, which is already causing problems around the world. We are only just beginning to learn the precise details of the damage that marine pollutants cause. Some of them are so toxic, or are present in such huge quantities, that they cause immediate death. Others are more subtle in their effects, but nonetheless may be responsible for weeks, months or even years of prolonged suffering. They gradually weaken the animals, causing hormonal imbalances, a lowering of disease resistance, cancer, and many other abnormalities and health problems, and may even cause a loss of fertility.

Despite all the warnings, many governments continue to pretend that the world's seas and oceans have an infinite capacity to absorb the waste products of human activities. Ever-increasing quantities of industrial waste, agricultural chemicals, radioactive discharges, untreated sewage, oil, modern plastic debris and a wide

1. A humpback whale snared in a salmon gill net off the coast of Newfoundland in Canada.

2. Huge amounts of waste are dumped into the sea every day. Here a ship is dumping industrial waste off the coast of Australia.

2

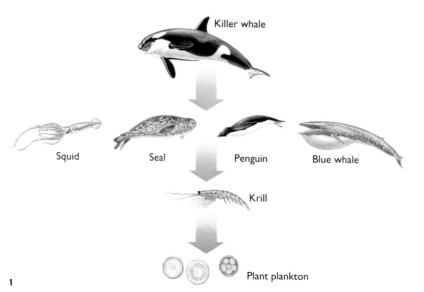

Killer whale

Squid   Seal   Penguin   Blue whale

Krill

Plant plankton

1

1. Killer whales are at the top of the food chain: in the Antarctic, for example, tiny planktonic plants are eaten by shrimp-like creatures called krill, which are eaten by squid, seals, penguins and baleen whales, and these in turn are eaten by killer whales.

2. The harm caused by noisy boats and ships, such as this cargo vessel, is largely unknown – but logic suggests that it is likely to be a serious problem.

variety of other pollutants are indiscriminantly dumped into the sea every day.

Unfortunately, killer whales and other top predators are particularly vulnerable to marine pollution, and recent studies have shown that they are now registering high levels of toxins in their bodies. This is because the toxins are permanently stored in fatty tissues and are readily passed along the food chain. Minute quantities are picked up by marine plankton, which are then eaten by fish and squid, and these in turn are eaten by the predators themselves. The higher up the food chain, the higher the concentration of toxins. Transient killer whales are hit particularly hard, no doubt because of their almost exclusive diet of marine mammals, which are one step higher up the food chain than the fish preyed upon by resident killer whales.

Worse still, much of this build-up is passed on to the next generation. Unborn calves absorb toxins through the bloodstream and, even after they have been born, continue to take in concentrated doses through their mothers' milk. Therefore, even before they start hunting, young killer whales may already have dangerously high levels of toxins in their bodies. By the time they reach adulthood, they are carrying many more pollutants for their body weight than most other cetaceans.

Noise pollution

The underwater world can be surprisingly noisy. Invertebrates, fish and marine mammals make a medley of different sounds: the low-frequency moans of blue and fin whales, for example, are so loud that they can be heard for thousands of kilometres. A variety of natural events, from underwater volcanic eruptions to heavy rain, add to the cacophony.

In recent years, though, human activities have added considerably to these natural sounds, and experts are concerned about their impact on marine life. Dredging, coastal development, speed boats, jet skis, heavy shipping such as tankers and container ships, low-flying aircraft, military manoeuvres, seismic testing for oil and gas exploration, drilling rigs, sonar and acoustic telemetry are all to blame for this noise pollution.

There has been relatively little research in this field, so the harm caused to killer whales and their relatives is largely unknown. It is particularly difficult to evaluate because it is not just the loudness of a noise that is important, but its frequency as well. Different species are believed to be more sensitive to some frequencies than others: in particular, large cetaceans to low frequencies and small cetaceans to higher ones.

But even without a great deal of research, logic suggests that killer whales are likely to be highly vulnerable to noise pollution. After all, they live in a world of sound and rely on effective hearing for communication, finding their way around and locating their prey. Indeed, there is a growing body of coincidental evidence to suggest that, as well as directly interfering with all these day-to-day

2

activities, extraneous noise may also have side effects such as reducing the animals' sensitivity to important sounds, or causing them unnaturally high levels of stress.

Habitat degradation and disturbance

One of the greatest threats to wildlife on land is habitat degradation and disturbance, whether it be tropical rainforest destruction, desertification, or building roads across important grasslands and heathland. Whales, dolphins and porpoises suffer from similar threats, although in different ways. Coastal and riverbank development, land reclamation, deep-sea dumping, oil, gas and mineral exploration, commercial fish farming, boat traffic and the effects of land-based activities such as deforestation and river damming are all to blame. Species living close to shore, or in rivers, tend to be the hardest hit – but the impact of these human activities can reach far out to sea as well. Their consequences can be quite subtle, such as increased amounts of sediment or changes in salinity, but they can also be dramatic. Habitat degradation along the coast, for example, can have a far-reaching impact on the marine environment as a whole, as this is where nurseries for fish and all kinds of other wildlife form the foundation of the sea's complex food webs.

Habitat protection

One long-term solution is to protect entire habitats. No matter how many laws and regulations are passed to protect whales, dolphins and porpoises, they will be useless if the animals have nowhere safe to live. Habitat protection means providing them with special sanctuaries, or marine reserves,

1. The mismanagement of coastal areas – such as here in Moreton Bay, Australia – is typical of our careless maltreatment of the marine environment.

2. People have surprisingly little respect for seas and oceans, and even treat beaches as rubbish dumps.

CARING FOR KILLER WHALES

There are so many potential threats that everyone involved in killer whale conservation feels a sense of despair and helplessness from time to time. But progress is being made, and the attitudes of governments and other key decision-makers are changing.

The work undertaken by a conservation organization such as the UK-based Whale and Dolphin Conservation Society (WDCS) is necessarily wide-ranging. WDCS's work includes everything from developing a good working relationship with key politicians to promoting a feeling of mutual respect and cooperation with local fishermen. It encourages schoolchildren to take an interest in whale conservation, and focuses world attention on key issues such as marine pollution, destructive fishing methods and killer whales in captivity. It produces action plans for saving endangered populations, and develops economic alternatives to hunting and killing. It also gathers information on illegal activities, improves the enforcement of existing laws and regulations, and tackles many other issues.

How you can help

Concerned individuals really can make a difference. You can help by joining a whale conservation group; supporting campaigns by writing letters of protest to politicians and other key decision-makers and by organizing petitions; raising money through sponsored activities, such as walks or parachute jumps; and by encouraging other people to take an active interest in killer whale conservation.

2

in which they are guaranteed long-term protection from habitat degradation and disturbance, as well as from hunting, destructive fishing methods and myriad other threats. Such reserves need to be sufficiently large to secure safe refuges in which the animals can feed and breed without having to enter more dangerous waters. Some marine sanctuaries already exist, such as the Southern Ocean Whale Sanctuary, which was established primarily for the baleen whales, and Robson Bight Ecological Reserve in Johnstone Strait, British Columbia, which is tiny in comparison but was established especially for killer whales. This form of marine conservation is still in its infancy, however.

FURTHER INFORMATION

BOOKS

The Conservation of Whales and Dolphins: Science and Practice, edited by Mark P. Simmonds and Judith Hutchinson (J. Wiley, 1996).

Guardians of the Whales: The Quest to Study Whales in the Wild, Bruce Obee and Graeme Ellis (Whitecap Books, 1992).

A Guide to the Photographic Identification of Individual Whales, Jon Lien and Steven Katona (American Cetacean Society, 1990).

Orca: The Whale Called Killer, Erich Hoyt (Firefly, 1990).

The Sierra Club Handbook of Whales and Dolphins, Stephen Leatherwood and Randall R. Reeves (Sierra Club Books, 1983).

Whales, Dolphins and Porpoises, Mark Carwardine (Dorling Kindersley, 1995).

Whales and Dolphins: The Ultimate Guide to Marine Mammals, Mark Carwardine, Erich Hoyt, R. Ewan Fordyce and Peter Gill (HarperCollins, 1998).

Killer Whales, John K.B. Ford, Graeme M. Ellis and Kenneth Balcombe (UBC Press, 2000).

Transients: Mammal-Hunting Killer Whales, John K.B. Ford and Graeme M. Ellis (UBC Press, 1999).

Whale Watching, edited by Nicky Leach (Discovery Communications, 1999).

MAGAZINE
BBC Wildlife Magazine
A monthly look at wildlife and conservation worldwide.

WEBSITES
American Cetacean Society
http://www.acsonline.org/

Whale and Dolphin Conservation Society
http://www.wdcs.org

Society for Marine Mammalogy
http://pegasus.cc.ucf.edu~smm

INDEX